HETZER

JAGDPANZER 38(t) and G-13

ONE OF THE MOST SUCCESSFUL GERMAN TANK DESTROYERS

HORST SCHEIBERT

Left:
Late version tank destroyer Pz 38(t). Its 75mm Pak 39 L/48 was the slightly modified Kampfwagenkanone (KwK) L/48 of the Panzer IV H. On the roof of the Hetzer is an armored dome that protected the periscope from the movements of the machine gun which was mounted to its right. Two armored shields protected the internally controlled MG (not mounted in photo).

Schiffer Publishing Ltd®
4880 Lower Valley Road Atglen, Pennsylvania 19310

SOURCES:
Kamptruppenschule 2 of the Bundeswehr
The Swiss Army

The archives of:
H.J. Schroeder
H. Scheibert
H.J. Nowarra
Podzun
Modell-Fan (Sketches)
Bundesarchiv Koblenz
and Mr. K. Sarrazin,
whom I would especially like to thank for his help and support.

Translated from the German by Paul Reinert.

This book originally published under the title,
Hetzer Jagdpanzer 38 (t) und G-13,
by Podzun-Pallas Verlag, GmbH, Markt 9, 6360 Friedberg,
© 1979. ISBN: 3-7909-0064-8.

Library of Congress Control Number: 90-60477.

ISBN: 978-0-88740-238-8
Printed in China

Published by Schiffer Publishing Ltd.
4880 Lower Valley Road
Atglen, PA 19310
Phone: (610) 593-1777; Fax: (610) 593-2002
E-mail: Info@schifferbooks.com

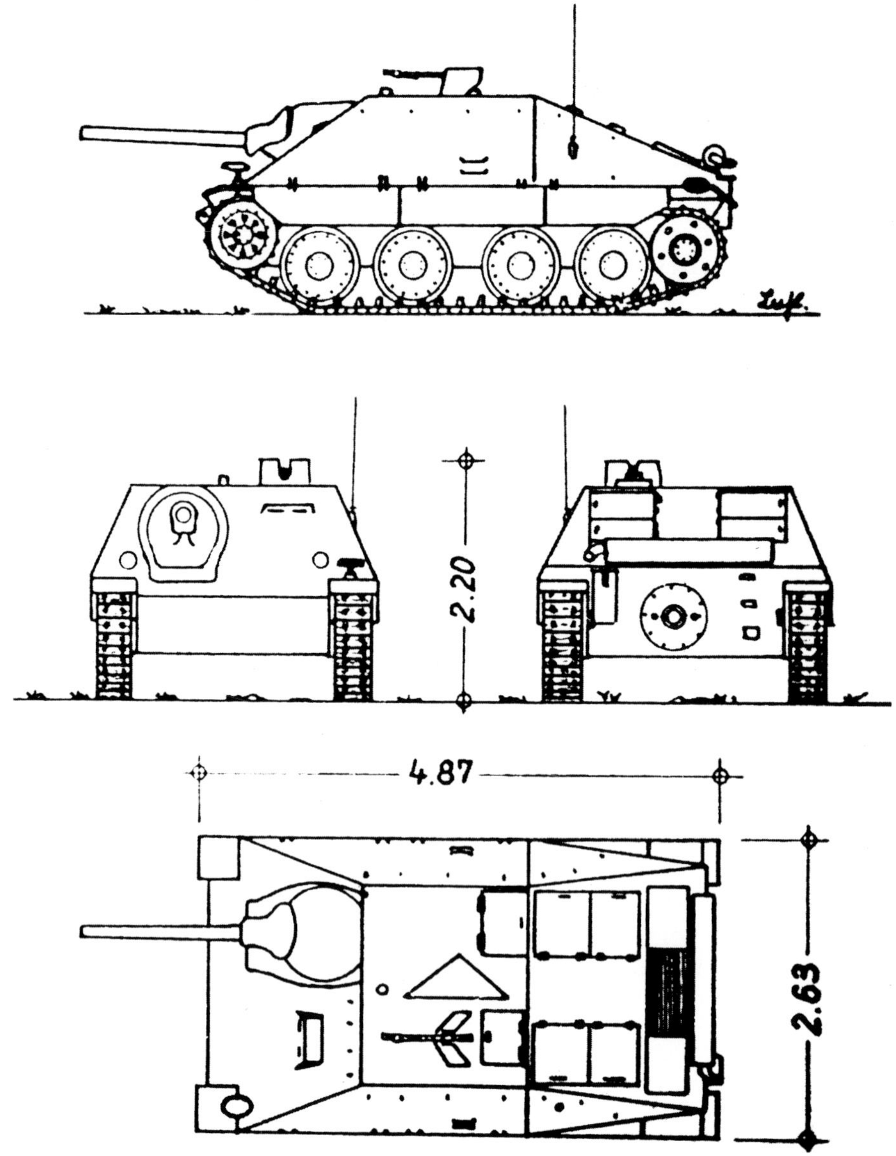

Line drawings of a Hetzer.

HETZER
Jagdpanzer 38(t)

The tank Destroyer was born out of necessity and was to be found in countless variations in the German Army during WWII. Whether improvised or ordered into production, all versions were built from the weapons and chassis on hand, either of German origin, or from captured war booty. They didn't have rotating turrets, and at first weren't as heavily armored as its tanks. Almost all early Panzerjagers showed some signs of improvising, thin armor and high silhouettes being two of their major weaknesses. These disadvantages were corrected in 1943 with the development of the Jagdpanzer IV-VI and the Hetzer.

Smaller size, lighter mobility, heavier armor, along with lower silhouettes (by mounting the gun through the nose plate), plus proven chassis and drives were the major characteristics of the newer models. These changes gave the Jagdpanzers the speed, mobility, and survivability which the earlier models didn't possess. In contrast to the Kampfpanzer 38(t), the Hetzer had heavier armor, its motor a higher output, and its newer tracks were wider. Its main gun was the 75mm Pak 39 L/48, and mounted on the roof was an internally controlled MG. In its tortoise shell like form, it somewhat resembled the later models of the Sturmgeschutz III.

With these newer improvements over the early Panzerjagers, the Hetzer was to prove itself a great success in battle during the hardest fought years of the war. It was to appear also in a flamethrower version but in a very limited quantity. In order to conceal it as such, the flame projector was fitted inside the standard 75mm gun. A recovery version (Bergepanzer) also existed in which the cannon was replaced by a winch.

Although it proved to be a great tank destroyer, the Hetzer's disadvantages cannot be overlooked however. Its small silhouette and very favorable sloping armor greatly reduced the interior room available for the crew and layout. This was a major problem that had to be overcome by the designers. Another major disadvantage was the limited traverse of the cannon, the Hetzer had the least traverse of all Panzerjagers. The gunner and loader were seated to the left side of the cannon, and the commander didn't have enough periscopes for observation. The Hetzer also entered the war too late (May '44), and in limited numbers, and so there were never enough of them for the Panzerjager battalions of the infantry divisions, despite a production of almost 1600 units.

Due to its design and successes during the war, and since its manufacturers in Skoda and Prague, in Czechoslovakia were still working, the Hetzer had another life after the war and was known as the G-13. The G-13 was to serve in the Czech, Swedish, and till the beginning of the 70's, the Swiss army. Its great design characteristics haven't been lost by the designers of today's tank destroyers.

Technical Data

Motor	Gasmotor Prague AC/2800
Cylinders	6
Bore x Stroke	110 x 136mm
Piston displacement	7754ccm
Output	160 ps
Torque	2800/min
Compression	1:7
Carburetor	2 solex 46 FNVP
Valves	side mounted on camshaft dive wheels to the front
Crankshaft supports	7
Cooling	water pump
Battery	12 volt
Power train	Motor in hull rear driven by 2 tracks
Transmission	Parge-Wilson tarpaulin power drive with 5 forward gears + 1 reverse
Undercarriage	
Superstructure	One piece chassis Superstructure without turret
Running gear	2 tracks each of 98 links Dive wheel to the front Idler wheel in the rear

PD 010 354

The same Hetzer is pictured on both pages. Shown is one of the earliest Hetzer versions with the crimped outer edge of the gun mantel, and the older Pz38(t) idler wheel with twelve holes. The antennae is mounted on a pedestal on the left side hull. Later models would mount their antennae on the right side, minus a large base. The gun's shield is also different from the production type, and one of few pictured with it.

This Hetzer is moving through a town somewhere in the Balkans and is one of the later versions. It has the later gun mantel with the early gun shield and the older idler wheel with twelve holes. It's gun mantel also has a thicker ring below the cannon than usual. The antennae is mounted on a small socket on the right hull side as was to become standard.

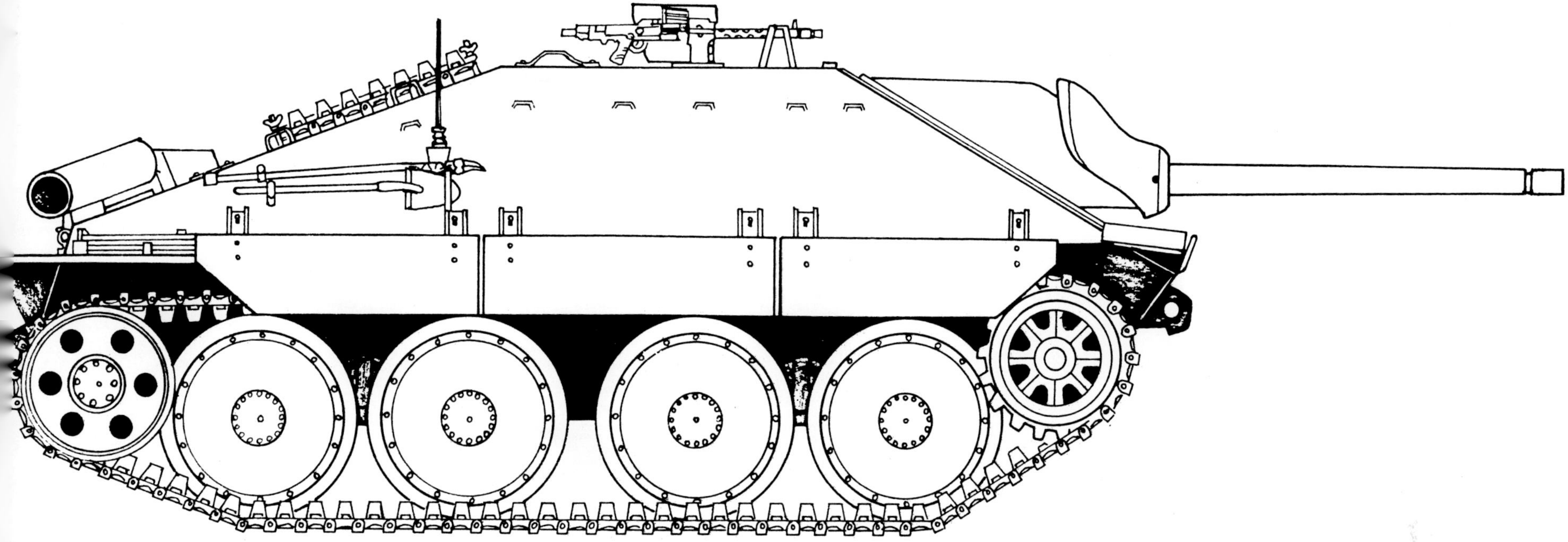

The line drawing above and picture at right show the Hetzer in it's most common production version with the newer idler wheel of six holes. Spare track links were usually kept on the rear roof. The seating for the crew was always a problem as in its layout there was barely enough seating provided inside, and unlike standard tanks there wasn't anyplace for riding on the outside.

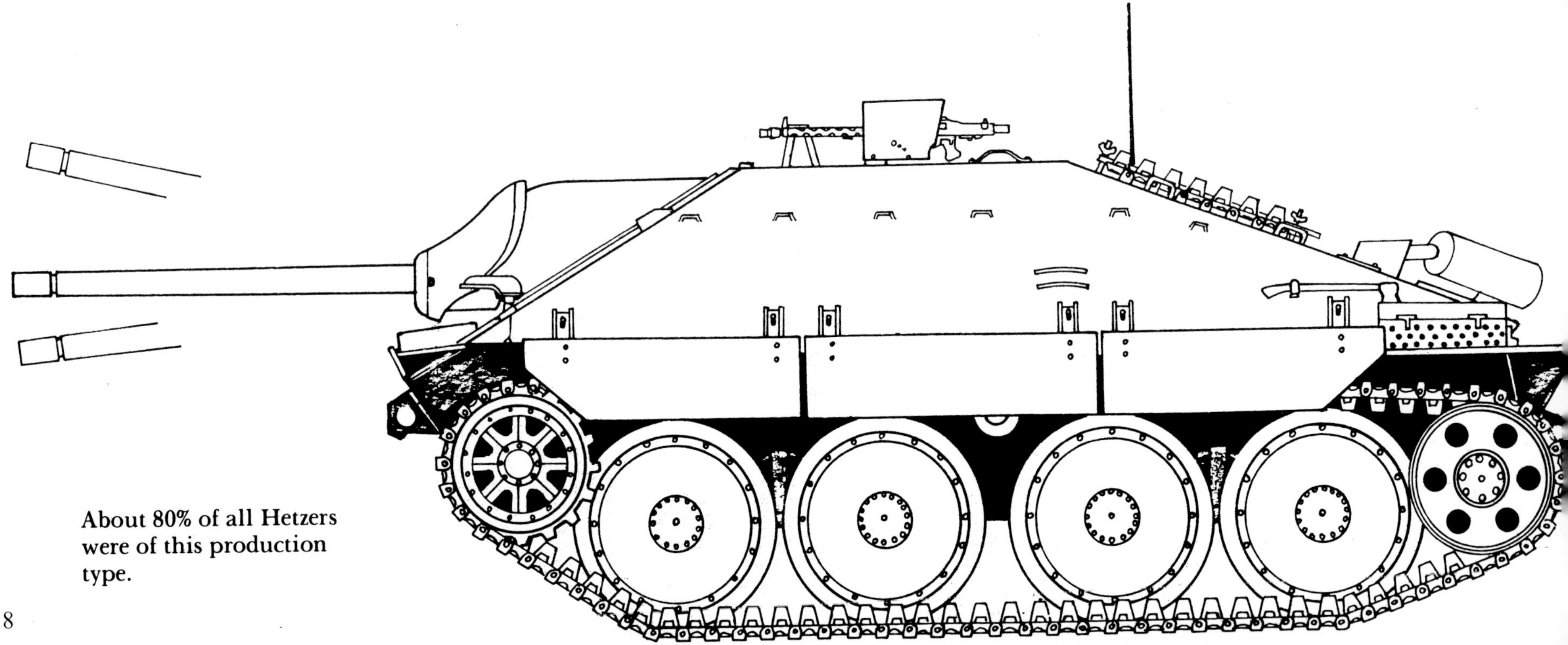

About 80% of all Hetzers were of this production type.

Steering and break system	**clutch-steering mechanism + mechanical steering break-steering operated by 2 levers**
Track length	**2690mm**
Track width	**350**
Size	**4870 x 2630 x 2170mm with cannon 6270mm**
Ground clearance	**420mm**
Water clearance	**1000m**
Turning radius	**5meters**
Combat weight	**16000kg**
Top speed	**42km/h**
Fuel consumption per 100km	**road 120 liters, country 180 liters**
Fuel storage	**320 liters**
Range	**road 260, country 170km**
Crew	**4 men**
Armor	**front 60mm, sides and rear 20mm**
Armament	**7,5 cm Pak 39 L/48 (41 rounds) + 1 MG experimental 7,5 cm KwK L/70 + 1MG**

Above: two Hetzers of the Waffen-SS in Lithuania during the winter of 1944/45.

Right: English soldiers inspecting a shot up Hetzer in a French village, fall 1944.

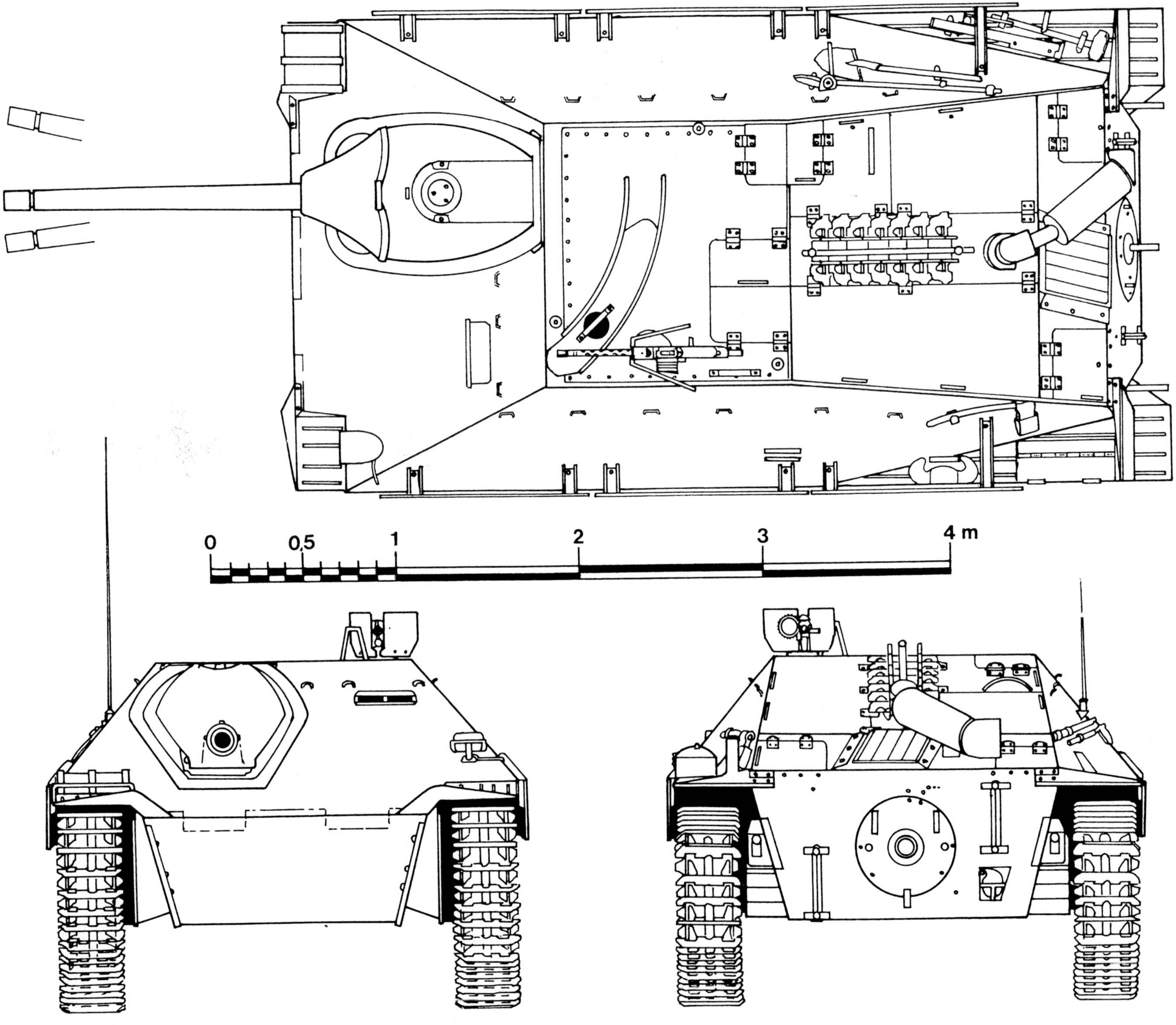
0
0,5
1
2
3
4 m

Left: The top drawing shows the protection given to the main armament. The lower right shows the sloping rear roof plate, and the removable armored plate for repairs to the motor which was taken from the Panzer 38(t).

Above: A birds eye view of a Hetzer currently in an English tank museum. The crews positions are shown clearly. Driver, gunner, loader, to the left in close quarters with the commander behind the cannon.

The same Hetzer as on the previous pages from different angles. The Hetzer was 50cm wider than the Panzer 38(t).

These two pictures show the two most common versions of the Hetzer.

Left: The same Hetzer again which is a later model. Right: Another Hetzer in a British museum but of an earlier type, recognizable by the idler wheel and mantel.

Left: An abandoned Hetzer captured by the Americans. Above another abandoned Hetzer which had an explosion in it's cannon barrel, inspected by a British soldier.

This Hetzer was abandoned in Morast, France (November 1944) after being stuck in the mud, it is a later version which has received some target practice as well. It is painted in the popular camouflage ambush pattern of light and dark spots reversed on light and dark backgrounds, common for all German vehicles (around mid '44) by brush.

In 1945 a few Hetzers received the longer 75mm Kwk 42 L/70 cannon of the "Panther", however, it proved to be too nose heavy and was discontinued. Despite its production of almost 1600, their are very few pictures of the Hetzer from German sources. This is attributed to the shortage of film in the later war years in Germany, so most pictures of the Hetzer in the field are of abandoned or knocked out vehicles from Allied sources. The others are of Hetzer's in museums.

Above left: A Flammpanzer 38(t), part of the barrel projector is in front of it in the snow. In the dummy barrel a smaller flame projector was mounted, this was to camouflage the vehicle and deceive the enemy as to it's use as a flamethrower tank.

Below: A burning Hetzer passed by an U.S. soldier with bazooka.

Three close up photo's showing the armored mount for the internally controlled MG. The same mounting was also used later in the war for the Sturmgeschute III.

The photo to the left shows the position of the MG just in front of the crew hatch. The sight for the MG was also housed in the mounting to the right side.

Jagdpanzer G-13 of the Swiss Army

After WWII the Swiss were able to buy 156 tank destroyers known as Jagdpanzer 38(t). Compared to the Hetzer little had changed—a muzzle brake was added, along with an idler wheel with four or eight holes instead of the Hetzers six or twelve. The internally controlled MG was removed and exchanged for a 360 degree periscope for the commander. The seating of the crew was also reversed, with the commander on the left side, and the gunner and loader on the right. Later, some received an observation port to the rear, and others were equipped with a light MG for close combat, mounted in the rear plating. Still others had two antennas and served as command vehicles, called Kommandopanzer in the Swiss army.

Known in the Swiss army as the G-13, it would equip the light brigades and later the field divisions up until the beginning of the 1970's. For use in the post war years it was also decided to change the motor to a Swiss manufactured diesel motor instead of the original Benzin motor.

Below:
A rare photo of a G-13 with the usual four holed idler wheel and muzzle brake, but with the internal MG and head lamp of a Hetzer.

The pictures here through page thirty, are all of G-13's as used by the Swiss army. They clearly show the differences as compared to the Hetzer. The absence of a MG on the roof, a four holed idler wheel and a muzzle break for the cannon, toolbox and spare track links, spare bogie mounted on the sides of the hull, commanders periscope, light MG and observation port on the rear plate are all apparent.

78003

Both pages show the same G-13 pictured. They clearly show the mounting of the light MG and the rearward facing periscope for the crew on the upper roof plating. This model is a Kommandopanzer as two antennae are mounted, and the commander's periscope is pointing to the right rear of the vehicle.

M-78082
13

Left:
This G-13 has a crew member observing towards the rear while traveling near Bern. It's head light has been turned around for unknown reasons, the cannon's sight for the gunner is easy to recognize in the mantel.

Above:
The same vehicle from different angles, interesting to note is the idler wheel here has eight holes in it.

Right: Close up of the mud guard and towing mechanism.

Left:
A command tank (Kommandopanzer) on maneuvers.

Above:
A good view of the reversed seating order of the G-13 as opposed to the Hetzer, which was better. In front of the commander under the "turning pot" is the main periscope.

Right:
A different Kommandopanzer without the MG 31, but in it's place reserve track links.

A G-13 with the typical reserve track links on the left side—on the right is a spare bogie. This G-13 has a hammer and axe on the left, and usually a jack was on the right side as well (it's base plate was stored on the front right mud guard). Some versions instead had a toolbox mounted where the hammer was.

This G-13 is in the outdoor museum of the Kampftruppenschule 2 of the Bundeswehr in Munster. The sign says that this is an original Hetzer with original markings which isn't true. It is a G-13 built in Pilsen—in 1971 the G-13's were replaced in the Swiss army by newer models. This is one of the early G-13's built, which had to do for the museum as an original Hetzer was not available.

All following photos through page 47 are of this and one other vehicle at theKampftruppenschule 2.

Top left: Are the gunners sighting optic which is coupled to the cannon, and the commander's periscope for all round view which is protected under the armored "pot."

Left: The observation port in the rear plate used by the crew.

Above: A view into the reel for the external phone minus its cable.

Close ups of the left front section of this G-13. The German Notek head lamp was mounted in Munster.

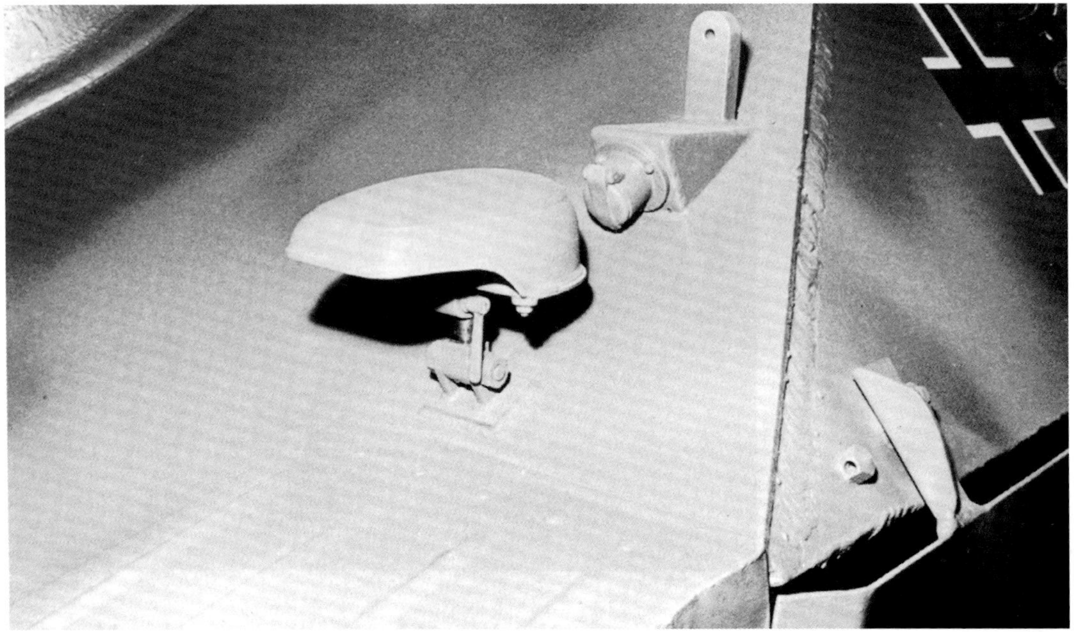

Above:
Two more shots of the G-13 in Munster. The newer Jagdpanzer of the Bundeswehr is in the background.

Left:
Close up of the Notek light. The Hetzer's power supply came directly from below—on the G-13 it came from the socket just above the lamp.

Right:
The drive and idler wheels.

The photos to the left and above show once again the small size, and well sloped armor of this Jagdpanzer.

Right: Pictured is the cannons 75mm muzzle brake, known in the Swiss army as the PAK 75mm.

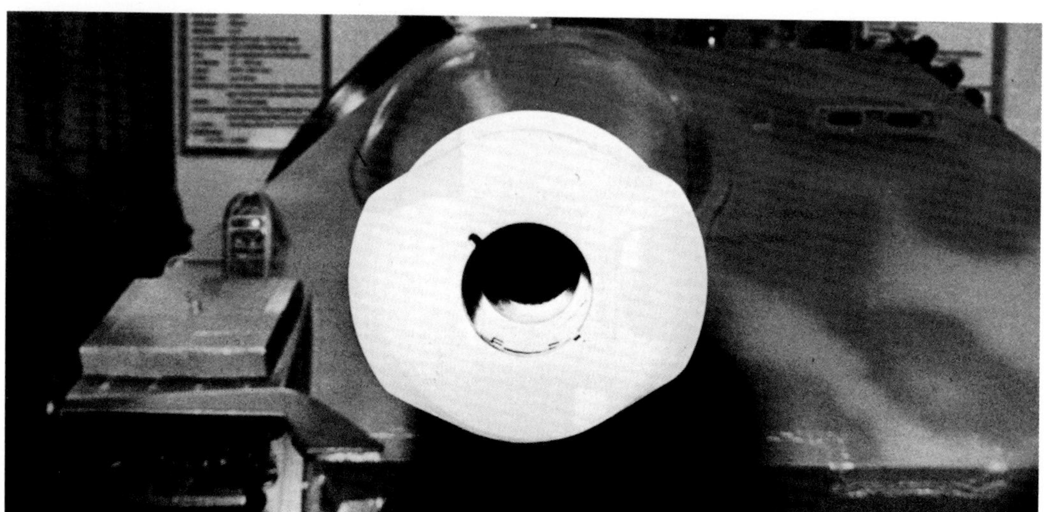

Above: The drivers vision port, and the gunners sight on the roof. All the photos on the right are detail shots of the cannon. The muzzle break had openings to the sides only, so as not to kick up ground dirt, this made it difficult however to observe the flight and impact of the shell.

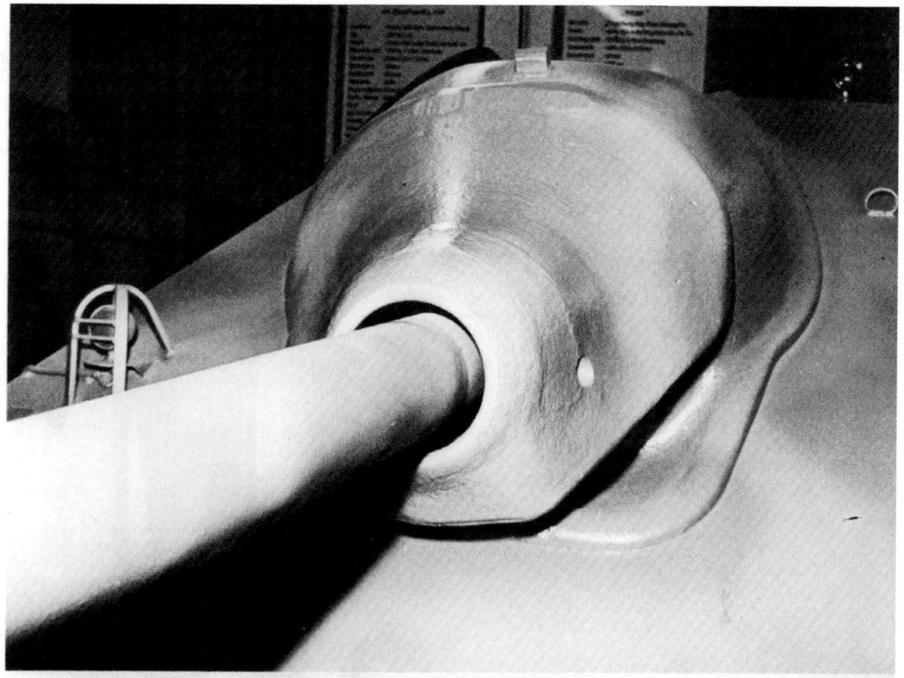
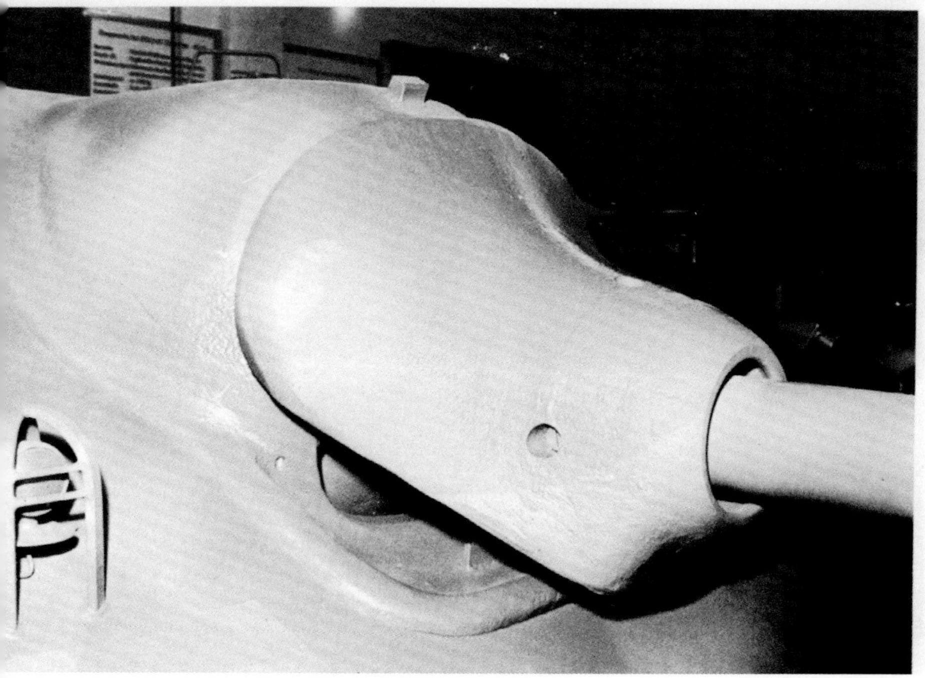
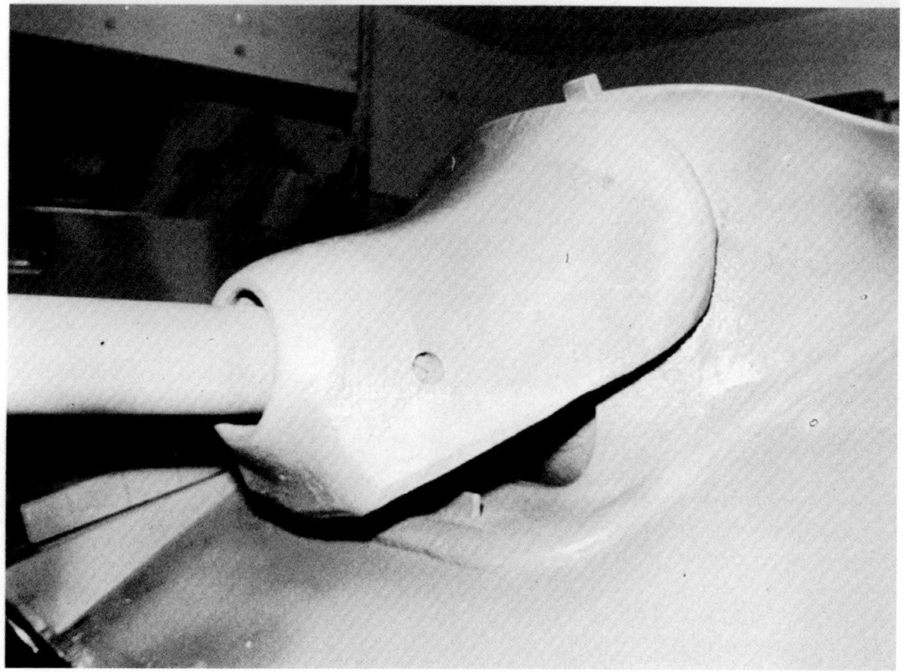

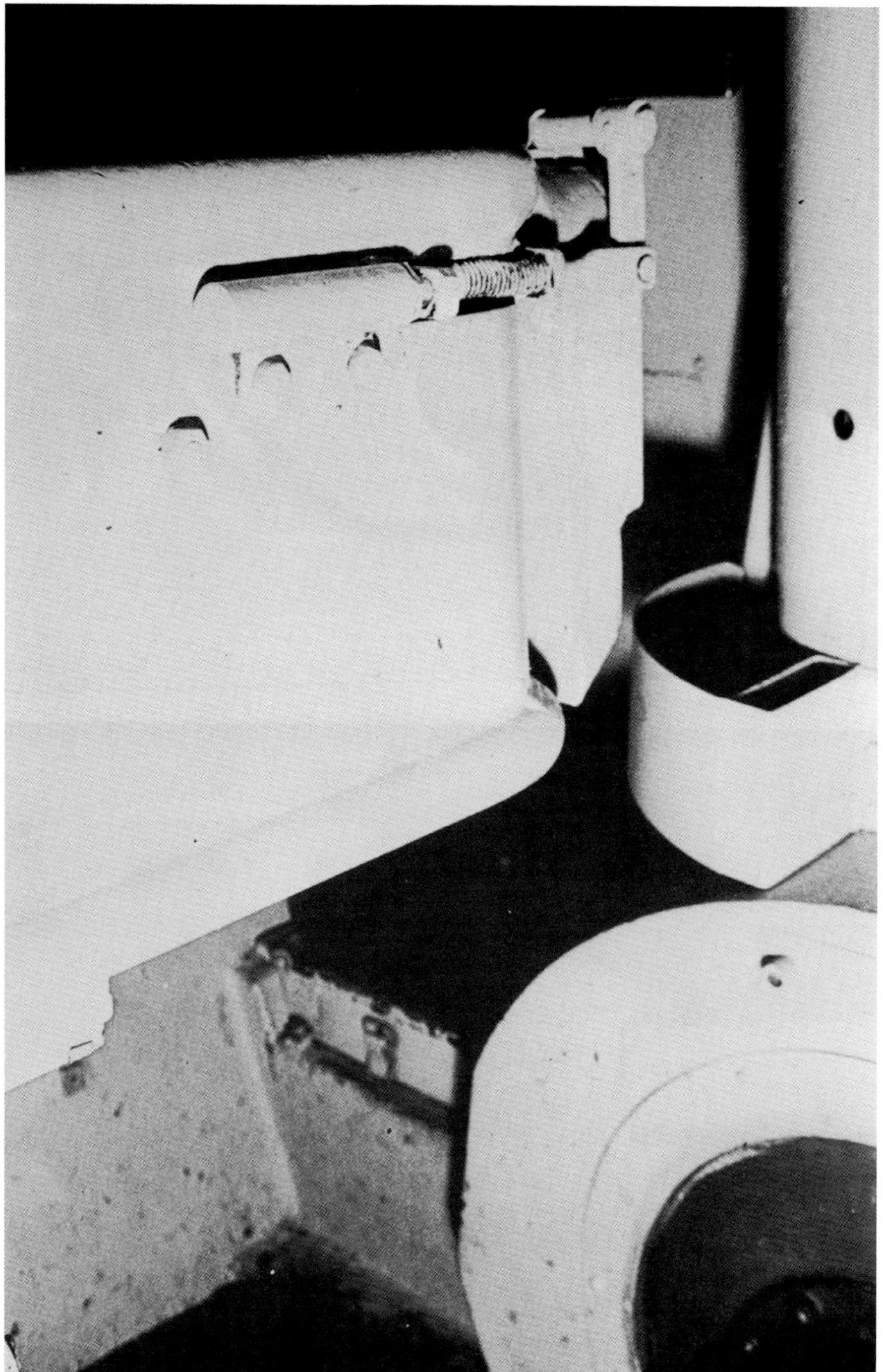

The picture above shows the most vulnerable area of the Hetzer (G-13), the area just below the cannon in the gun mantel. The pictures at the left show the hull from the inside motor area to the drive shaft, at far left is the cannons recoil guard with the cannon just visible at the end.

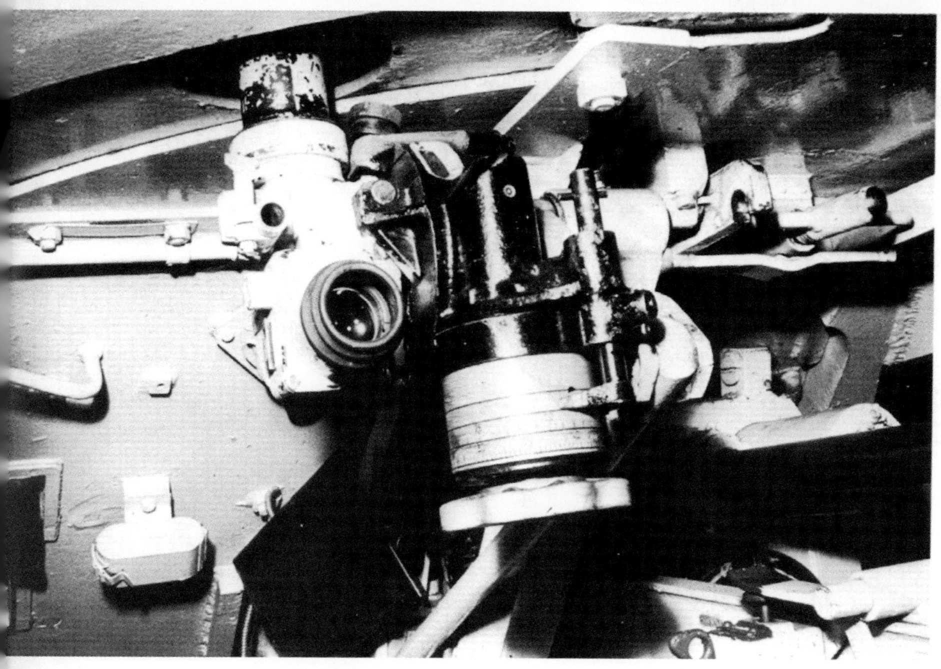

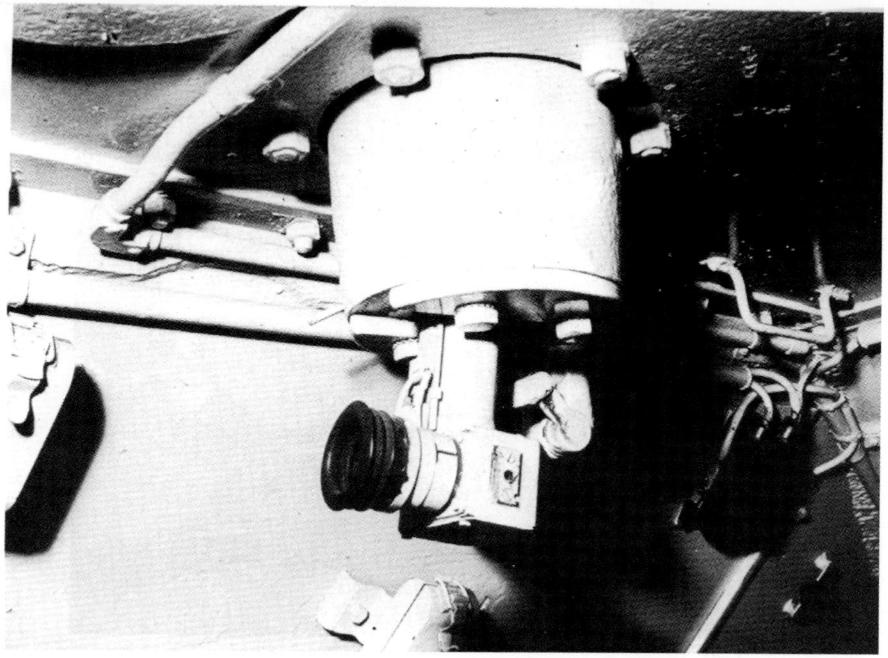

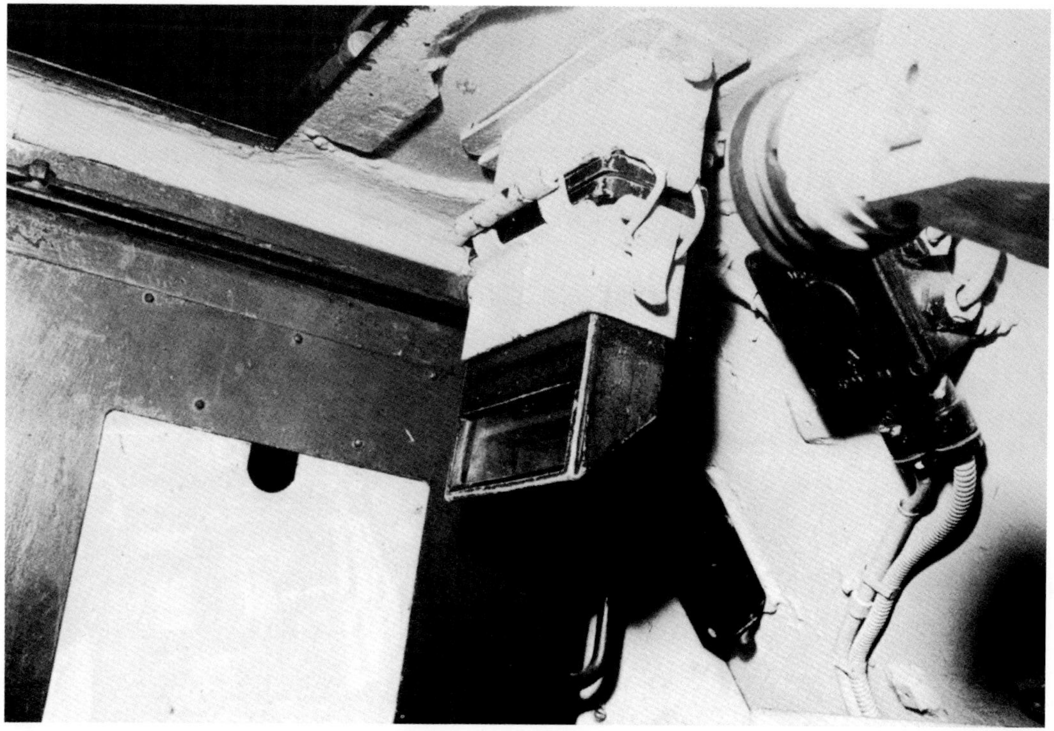

Left:
A good view of the G-13's optics for both the commander and gunner, the gunner's optic was coupled to the cannon and traversed in it's own armored plated section in the groove as shown here. The commanders periscope was housed in an armored dome which could rotate 360 degrees.

Above: The same two optics as seen from the inside—the gunner's periscope above and the commander's top right.

Right: The periscope for observing behind the vehicle which is mounted in the rear plate—the bulkhead for the engine compartment is also shown.

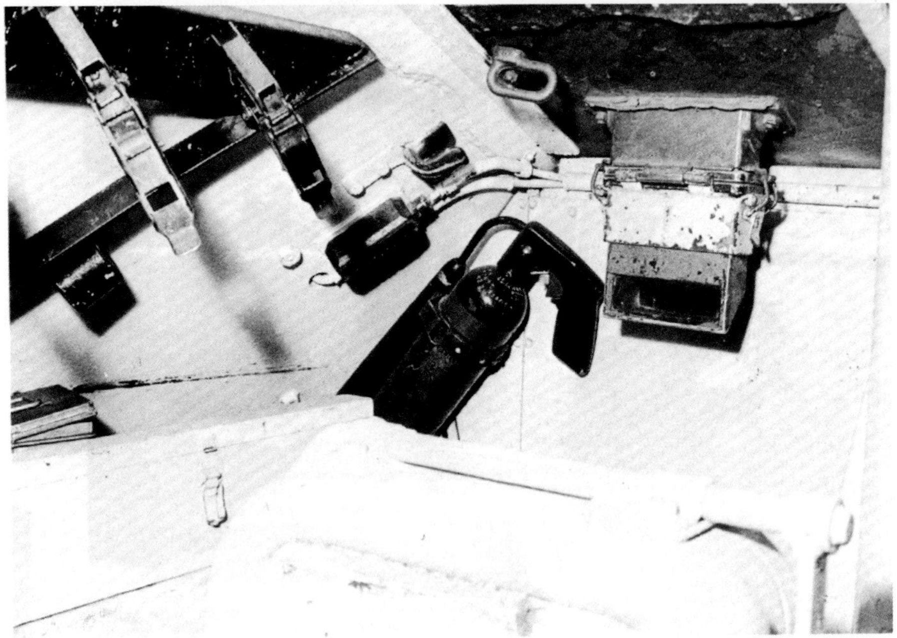

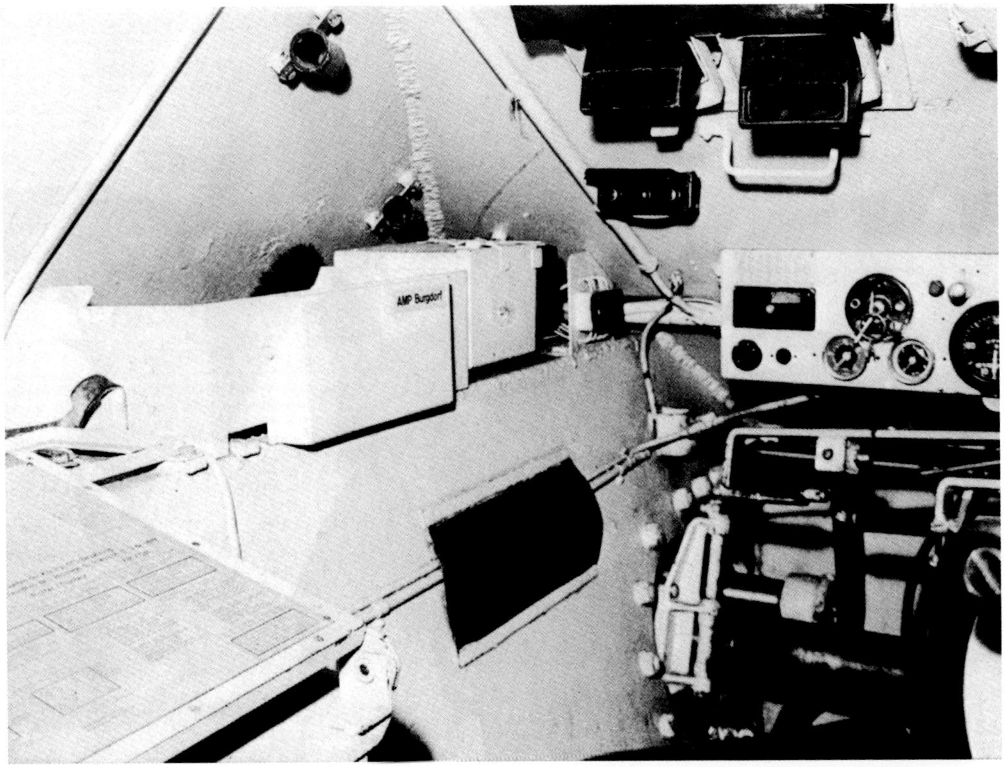

Top left:
The gunner's adjustments for gun laying, to the left is the azimuth (15 degrees per azimuth) control, with the elevation control at right.

Above:
A look rearward from the gun, the periscope for observation to the rear is pictured.

Left:
The left side of the drivers position.

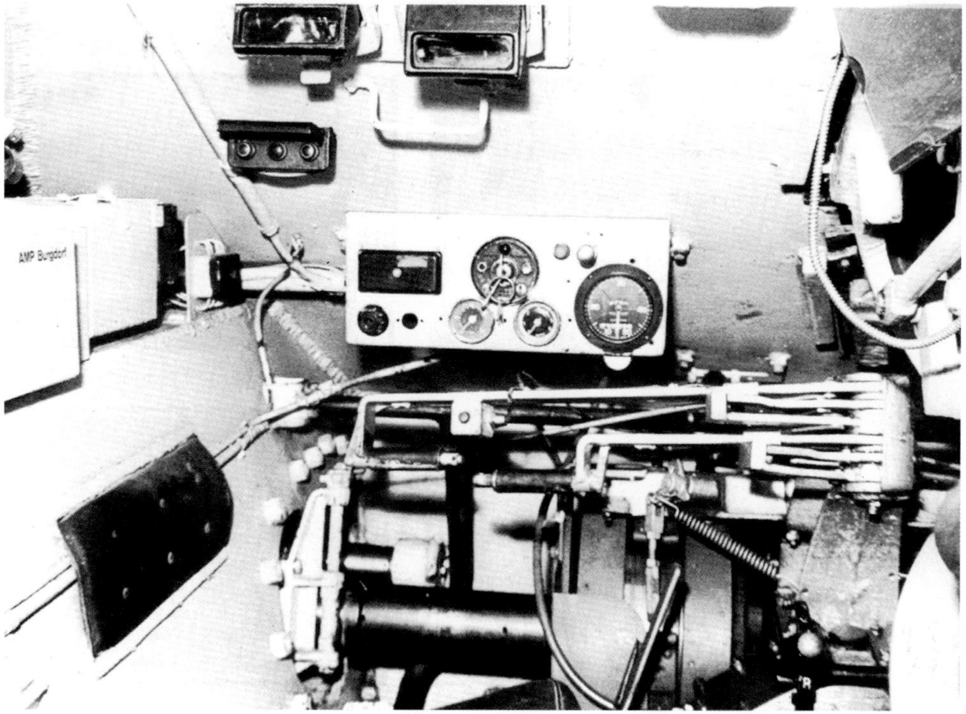

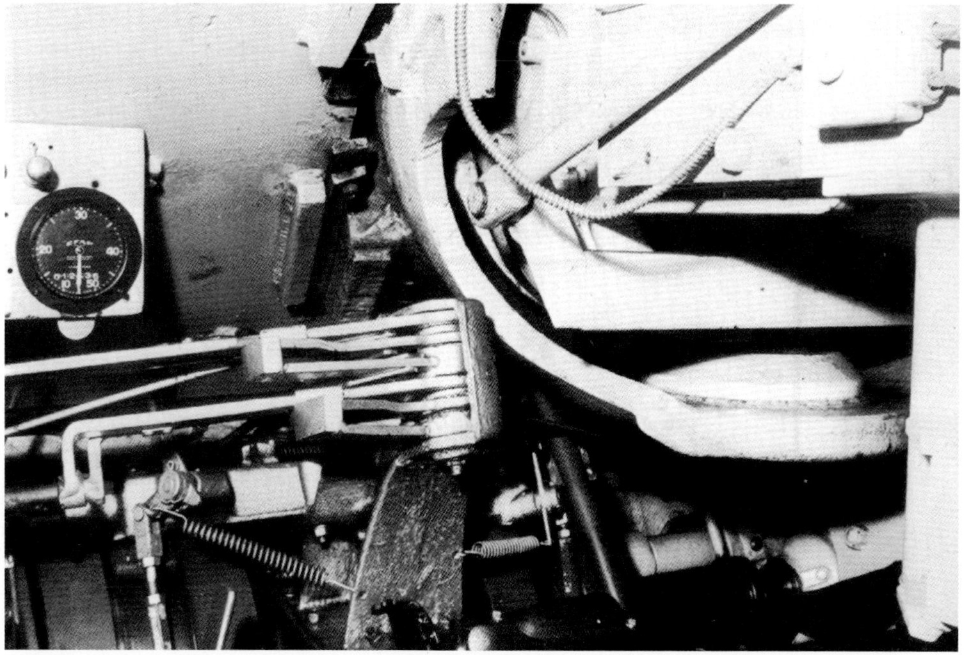

Above: The drivers seat and front part of the drive shaft and transmission.

Above right: The drivers position as seen from the commander's seat.

Right: the rightmost part of the driver's area, and the gun cradle is also visible.

ALSO FROM:

•SCHIFFER MILITARY HISTORY•

•THE WAFFEN-SS•THE HG PANZER DIVISION•
•THE 1ST SS ARMORED DIVISION•
•THE 12TH SS ARMORED DIVISION•

AND MORE...